EXTREMELY Weird ANIMALS
ELEPHANT SEAL

BY LISA OWINGS

BELLWETHER MEDIA • MINNEAPOLIS, MN

Jump into the cockpit and take flight with Pilot books. Your journey will take you on high-energy adventures as you learn about all that is wild, weird, fascinating, and fun!

This edition first published in 2014 by Bellwether Media, Inc.

No part of this publication may be reproduced in whole or in part without written permission of the publisher. For information regarding permission, write to Bellwether Media, Inc., Attention: Permissions Department, 5357 Penn Avenue South, Minneapolis, MN 55419.

Library of Congress Cataloging-in-Publication Data

Owings, Lisa.
  Elephant Seal / by Lisa Owings.
     pages cm. – (Pilot. Extremely Weird Animals)
  Summary: "Engaging images accompany information about elephant seals. The combination of high-interest subject matter and narrative text is intended for students in grades 3 through 7"– Provided by publisher.
  Audience: Ages 7-12.
  Includes bibliographical references and index.
  ISBN 978-1-62617-074-2 (hardcover : alk. paper)
  1. Elephant seals–Juvenile literature. I. Title.
  QL737.P64O95 2014
  599.79'4–dc23
                        2013037209

Printed in the United States of America, North Mankato, MN.

TABLE OF CONTENTS

FIGHTING FOR FEMALES

A huge male elephant seal hauls himself out of the ocean and onto a sandy beach. He is not here to relax. It is **breeding** season, and he must compete for mates. The beach soon becomes crowded with dozens of female elephant seals. This male wants them all to himself. When a younger male flops toward him, he raises his head in warning. He puffs out his dangling nose and lets out a loud roar.

The younger male does not back down. He is ready to fight. The two **bulls** rear up with open mouths. They slash at each other's scarred necks with their sharp teeth. The younger male is no match for the big, strong bull that first claimed the beach. He soon gives up and slinks away. The **alpha** male returns to his group of females.

ELEPHANTS OF THE SEA

Elephant seals are named for their trunk-like noses and massive size. They are the largest seals in the world. The two species of elephant seals are the northern elephant seal and the southern elephant seal. The southern elephant seal is the true giant. Males can weigh up to 8,800 pounds (4,000 kilograms) and measure up to 20 feet (6 meters) long. The largest male northern elephant seals weigh more than 4,500 pounds (2,040 kilograms). They can reach lengths of up to 16 feet (5 meters). Females of both species are much smaller.

Elephant seals are pinnipeds. This group of mammals includes seals, sea lions, and walruses. All pinnipeds have a thick layer of fat called blubber. Their blubber keeps them warm in the cold ocean. Elephant seals have small flippers and no visible ears. They have to wriggle on their bellies to move on land. These traits make them part of a group called "true seals."

Chomp! The only predators that can chomp through an elephant seal's blubber are great white sharks and killer whales.

human

elephant seal

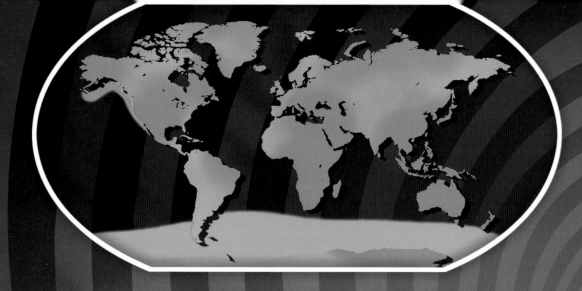

northern elephant seal range =
southern elephant seal range =

Narrow Noses

Angustirostris means "narrow nose." Northern elephant seals have this scientific name because they have thinner snouts than southern elephant seals.

Long ago, there was just one group of elephant seals. Scientists are not sure what caused the group to split in two. They only know that each species **adapted** to life in a different place. The southern elephant seal feels at home in Antarctic waters. It spends most of its days in the icy waters around the south pole. Its breeding grounds are the islands surrounding Antarctica.

The northern elephant seal flourishes in the northern Pacific. During most of the year, the northern elephant seal moves around the Pacific Ocean. It breeds mainly on small islands off the coasts of California and western Mexico.

Elephant seals spend most of their lives in the deep ocean. For eight to ten months each year, they repeatedly dive in search of food. They can stay underwater for up to two hours at a time. Between dives, they spend just minutes at the surface. Elephant seals eat mainly squid and deep-sea fish. They often travel many thousands of miles to get enough to eat. Northern elephant seals make the longest journeys. They swim up to 21,000 miles (33,800 kilometers) each year.

Elephant seals come together on land for breeding and **molting**. Each winter, males compete to mate with groups of up to 100 females. In summer, the seals stay on land for about a month to shed and regrow their coats. During this time, they lie close together and sleep. Their new coats grow in silvery gray. They later fade to brown.

molting

New Life

Elephant seal pups are born with thick, dark fur. This coat keeps them warm until their mother's milk fattens them up. Pups can pack on more than 200 pounds (91 kilograms) in their first month of life.

GETTING NOSY AND DIVING DEEP

A male elephant seal's nose begins to grow when he is two or three years old. Over time, it can reach up to 2 feet (0.6 meters) long. Males show off their noses during breeding. They puff them up by flexing certain muscles. They might also fill their noses with air or extra blood flow. This helps males appear bigger and more **threatening** to other males. It also makes their roars sound louder and deeper.

The male elephant seal's nose also helps him **conserve** water in his body. When an elephant seal breathes out, special passages in his nose trap some of the air. The warm air cools and forms water droplets, like breath on a window. The seal then **absorbs** the moisture back into his body.

Make It Short

An elephant seal can pull its nose back to show another male it means no harm or to protect its nose while fighting.

chest shield

Male elephant seals have thick skin around their necks. These chest shields start developing around the same time their noses begin growing. These protect the seals during fierce battles for mates. The skin becomes thicker and more scarred as the males grow older and survive more fights. In northern elephant seals, the chest shield looks pinkish. It is less noticeable in southern elephant seals.

Some of the elephant seal's most interesting features help it adapt to ocean life. Elephant seals spend nearly all their time underwater while at sea. Yet like humans, they breathe air. Instead of storing oxygen in their lungs, elephant seals store most of it in their blood. They have around twice as much blood as other large mammals. Elephant seals collapse their lungs before diving. This keeps them from getting **decompression sickness**. It also helps them sink more easily.

Elephant seals also use less oxygen and energy while underwater. One way they do this is by slowing down their heart rate. During a long dive, an elephant seal's heart may beat as few as four times per minute. Elephant seals also change the way their blood flows during dives. They keep it flowing only to the most important organs.

All of these changes happen as soon as the elephant seal begins to dive. It is an automatic response, like kicking when the doctor hits your knee. The **mammalian diving reflex** kicks in when cold water hits the seal's face. Its heart rate quickly drops. Its blood flows toward its brain and away from its skin and flippers. Entire areas of its body shut down to save energy. All mammals have some form of this reflex. Even humans do!

Into the Deep

Elephant seals dive deeper than almost any other mammal. They sometimes plunge more than a mile (1.6 kilometers) below the surface!

Light does not travel deeper than about 660 feet (200 meters) in the ocean. That means elephant seals must find most of their food in the dark. Their large eyes are very sensitive to light. Their eyes also have layers that reflect and magnify light from the surface or from prey that glow in the dark water. Seawater can harm elephant seals' eyes. During dives, their eyes are protected by **nictitating membranes**. These clear eyelids also keep their eyes moist and clean while on land.

Finding time to sleep is another challenge for elephant seals. Other ocean mammals spend time resting near the surface, but elephant seals rarely stop diving. They appear to nap while they dive. They swim down past where most predators live, then drift like falling leaves to the ocean floor. Sometimes they hit the bottom before waking!

Hold Your Breath

Elephant seals' noses stay closed while they are resting. This keeps the animals from drowning. Even when sleeping on land, seals often hold their breath.

SAVED FROM EXTINCTION

Elephant seals have been hunted for food for thousands of years. In the 1800s, people began killing them in large numbers for their blubber. The blubber was made into oil. In the 1900s, laws were passed to protect surviving seals. Since then, elephant seals have made a major comeback. Both species are now listed as least concern. That means they have a low risk of dying out.

However, populations in some areas have dropped by as much as half. Scientists believe overfishing may have made food **scarce**. **Climate change** may also be to blame. Humans must do what they can make sure these giants keep showing off their noses and exploring the deep seas.

EXTINCT
EXTINCT IN THE WILD
CRITICALLY ENDANGERED
ENDANGERED
VULNERABLE
NEAR THREATENED
LEAST CONCERN

Elephant Seal Fact File

Common Name:	northern elephant seal; southern elephant seal
Scientific Name:	Mirounga angustirostris; Mirounga leonina
Famous Feature:	long, trunk-like nose
Distribution:	Pacific waters along the coasts of California and Baja California; Antarctic waters
Habitats:	deep sea, sandy beaches
Diet:	squid, fish, octopuses, small sharks, rays, other deep-sea animals
Life Span:	9 years for northern elephant seals; 20 years for southern elephant seals.
Current Status:	least concern

GLOSSARY

absorbs—soaks up or takes in

adapted—changed over time to adjust to a new situation

alpha—dominant or in charge

blubber—a thick layer of fat under the skin of pinnipeds

breeding—mating to produce young

bulls—male elephant seals

climate change—a long-lasting change in weather patterns; climate change is often traced to burning fossil fuels like oil and coal.

conserve—to save something from being lost or wasted

decompression sickness—the formation of bubbles in the body after moving too quickly from high-pressure to low-pressure surroundings; decompression sickness occurs in human divers and can be deadly.

mammalian diving reflex—a reaction that happens when cold water touches a mammal's face; the mammalian diving reflex includes slowed heart rate and changed blood flow.

mammals—animals that have backbones, hair, and feed their young milk

molting—losing hair, feathers, or layers of skin; elephant seals shed their fur and top layer of skin all at once.

nictitating membranes—clear eyelids that close to protect an elephant seal's eyes

pinnipeds—mammals that eat meat, live in the water, and have flippers; pinnipeds include seals, sea lions, and walruses.

scarce—limited in quantity

threatening—showing signs of being dangerous or harmful

TO LEARN MORE

AT THE LIBRARY

Goldish, Meish. *Southern Elephant Seal: The Biggest Seal in the World*. New York, N.Y.: Bearport Pub., 2010.

Malam, John. *Pinnipeds*. New York, N.Y.: Franklin Watts, 2010.

Throp, Claire. *Seals*. Chicago, Ill.: Heinemann Library, 2013.

ON THE WEB

Learning more about elephant seals is as easy as 1, 2, 3.

1. Go to www.factsurfer.com.

2. Enter "elephant seals" into the search box.

3. Click the "Surf" button and you will see a list of related Web sites.

With factsurfer.com, finding more information is just a click away.

INDEX

The images in this book are reproduced through the courtesy of: Dominic Laniewicz, front cover; Ai Angel Gentel/ Getty Images, p. 5; Peter Bassett/ Nature Picture Library, p. 7; Minden Pictures/ SuperStock/ Masterfile, pp. 8-9, 10-11; Visuals Unlimited, Inc./ Solvin Zankle/ Getty Images, p. 10; Eduardo Rivero, p. 13; Radius Images/ Glow Images, pp. 14-15; NHPA/ SuperStock, pp. 16-17; Animals Animals/ SuperStock, pp. 18-19; Wayne Lynch/ Glow Images, p. 21.